The Store is Open

By

Trent Andrews

"A simple mind thinks inside the box.

An interesting mind thinks outside the box.

A wonderful mind created the box."

Trent

CONTENTS

Hate is Hate

Hate is a disease: How often do you hear about a woman who allows herself to be beaten by her husband multiple times? And yet, she continues to remain in the relationship. Does she think it's normal because she has seen the same behavior towards her mother by her father? A man strikes his wife. Why? Did he learn this from his father as a child? Did the man and woman contract the hate disease carried by their parents? What is the cure?

Hate is the Dark Sun: My wife hates Donald Trump so much that she turns the TV to another channel whenever he appears on the News. She sometimes walks out of the room or uses profanity just by looking at him. She doesn't realize the "Hate Rays" radiating from her. Hate Rays don't give warmth like the rising Sun in the morning. Hate Rays doesn't nurture positive growth, unlike the life-giving light our Sun provides to all living things. Hate Rays only torch those around it, leaving burns of anger. If you look at the Dark Sun, your "positive" eyes will surely go blind.

Hate is ignorance: These A-rabs are buying up everything in the neighborhood. Shew! I know these White folks got money. She must be on welfare. You look suspicious. You're a credit to your race. They all look alike to me. We don't serve your kind. You don't belong in this neighborhood. Taxi, taxi…taxi!

Hate is jealousy, envy, and greed: Think about it. Everything we do that leads to hurting someone is the result of hating something else. For example, if you rob a bank or person, most likely you hate being without money. If you kill someone, most likely you hate what they did or who they are.

Hate is pain: The pain we cause. The pain we receive. The hurt we cause. The hurt we receive. The sadness we cause. The sadness we receive. The suffering we cause. The suffering we receive.

Hate is hated.

Spirituality

What exactly is it? Where did it come from? Is it real? Do we all have it? What makes us humans believe in something we cannot see, hear, or touch?

As a species we humans have many physical things in common; Two eyes, two arms, two legs, a brain, a heart, and so forth. We also have a spirituality, which is a commonality that all mankind share.

For thousands of years, man has looked to the sky to worship celestial objects. The Romans and Greeks named stars, planets, and constellations after Gods they believe existed on Mount Atlas. The ancient Indigenous tribes believed they were able to connect to the pagan Gods of Mother Earth. The Egyptians had their Gods, the Europeans had their Gods, the Asians had their Gods, even the Aztek and Inkas had their Gods. Yet, for a vast period of time, none of these civilizations knew the other existed. So how could mankind, in all areas of the world have the same practice of worshiping a higher being? Is it mankind's instinct to create what our limited knowledge cannot explain? If so, is superstition a part of man's basic instincts, such as love and fear? Or, is spirituality something that connects us in this realm and the next? Unlike a physical tool, is religion the mechanism used to tap into spirituality? Or, is religion the mechanism used to distort or distance man away from spirituality?

I believe spirituality is a personal journey that does not require a lifetime of guidance from another's point of view. Some find it in different areas of their life. It might be found during meditation or prayer. Or, it might be found while you're walking alone on a sunny day in the park. Spirituality is strength. Spirituality is beautiful. Spirituality is peace. Spirituality is me. Spirituality in you.

The New Woke

We are in a battle. A battle for our survival regarding where we come from, and where we're going. Some may argue, our direction to the future is no longer based on free will. It's based on those who oppose us as influential Americans, free-thinking Americans who happen to be Black Americans. We did not purchase any cruise tickets to board that Trans-Atlantic slave ships that brought us to the new land. We did not select that fancy metal jewelry that bound our hands and feet together during the cruise. Unlike the Europeans, we did not migrate in droves to find our fame and fortune. Died, survived, and thrived, is our story.

From the United Daughters of the Confederacy to Florida's Governor Ron DeSantis, Black history has been under attack. There were no, and are no, heroes that waved the Confederate battle flag fighting for the survival of slavery. There aren't any "truth-seeking" scholars that want to eliminate history and replace it with political extremist rhetoric. In 2023, Governor DeSantis banned all AP African American studies in the state of Florida. Yet, he did not ban any AP Hispanic studies, AP Asia studies, or AP European studies. And the funny thing about it, is AP African American studies are American studies, hence the word "American."

Remember when the New Jersey Black high school student (Andrew Johnson) was forced to cut his dreadlocks prior to his wrestling match? His coach ordered one of his staff to cut the young man's hair in front of the entire auditorium. What about the Texas student who was barred from attending classes and graduation unless he cut his locs? What about the young Black gymnast female in Ireland who was passed over during the metal ceremony? Every young gymnast team member received a metal, except her.

There's a Netflix series called; Orange is the New Black. Is "woke" the new Jim Crow? Is freedom of speech belittling others the new Woke? Is American awoke?

Words

You know, the biggest lie in the world, besides Jesus was a white man with blond hair and blue eyes. Is "Sticks and stones will break my bones, but names will never hurt me." That might have been true many years ago, but not today.

I learned last week some words can offend someone without you even knowing. I used the word "that" to describe a person. I didn't realize it was the same as saying "those people." Some words can mean one thing to one person and another thing to someone else. We use words like "cool" to describe the weather or a person's charismatic personality. You hear some women call men "dogs." Most men brush it off. But if we (men) call a woman a "bitch" which is a female dog. Watch out! All hell's going to break loose.

In your life, you probably have cut your finger with a kitchen knife. It hurts for a moment and eventually heals with or without a scar. But the invisible knife call hurtful words, jabs at the heart and cuts through the soul, which can leave an everlasting wound that may never heal.

Would a word offend you if you didn't know the meaning? How do you know you weren't cussed out in Chinese at a Chinese restaurant because you complained about your order? Remember when your child got angry at you, turned to walk away, and mumbled under his or her breath? You replied. "What did you say?" You wanted to hear the words that you knew would make you angry. Funny, isn't it? You wanted to hear the words that jab at your heart.

Maybe we need both? The words that sooth us and the words that ruffle our feathers. Maybe it's the balance? The Yin and Yang. The dark and the light. The truth and the lie. Maybe without one, you don't have the other?

African American

I saw a White guy on TV that was born and raised in Johannesburg, South Africa. He migrated to the United States to become a U.S. citizen. When he was asked, what is your nationality? He replied, African American. When you think about it, by definition, he is more of an African American on paper, than Blacks in America who identify themselves as African American.

Why do Blacks in American identify themselves today as African Americans? I once heard that "we" should identify ourselves as such because our ancestor linear heritage comes from Africa. At which some other races identify themselves based on their Motherland. For example; the Irish would say Irish-American, the Italians would say Italian-American.

However, you don't see White Americans whose heritage dates back to early Europe calling themselves anything but Americans. I never seen any official documentation related to employment or school entry that has a box to check for those identifications. Black people born and raised in Cuba call themselves Cubans. Blacks in Jamaica call themselves Jamaicans. Surely their ancestors were taken from African as slaves as well. Yet here "we" are committing ourselves too African American.

I believe by using the term African American separate ourselves from the accomplishments we made to build this country. What I mean by this, is that using the word African somehow connects all our skills and triumphs to the continent of Africa. As if we are not Americans first. Our ancestors born and raised in America fought hard for us to have "equal" rights on every level. To live where we want, to eat where we want, and to be educated where we want. Just like any other American living in the land. It wasn't African heritage that made the Tuskegee Airman successful, it wasn't African heritage that pushed for voting rights. It was the courage we build living in a land that enslaved us and denied us the basic human rights that all people should have.   Dr. Martin Luther King was an American, Malcolm X was an American, Harriet Tubman was an American. Let's not take that away from them. Oh yeah, I'm an American.

The Experiment

Some say America is not a country but an experiment. It was intended to be the only country on Earth where multiple cultures and languages can come together and live as one. Sharing the same goals and aspirations. Acting as one when our values and way of living are threatened by outside forces. Is the American experiment coming to the end? Is the experiment a failure or success? I guess the real question is, what is America?

We call ourselves the United States of America which means there must be a separation between the States to unite. America has fifty different individual territories and more than fifty different ways to govern the people. In one State you can carry a gun openly, while in another you can't. Some states have the death penalty, while others do not. And what about the abortion issue? Good luck, ladies! Rules and laws passed by individual state's legislative bodies can dictate a person's lifestyle differently, yet we call ourselves the "United" States. Some even say, that the federal government which unites us as a country, has overreached into state's affairs, and that there is too much federal government involvement when it comes to state's decisions on how to govern.

We claim to be the world's leader in democracy, yet the Electoral College overrules the popular vote when electing a President. Our two-party system has pretty much blocked any chance for any other party to control Congress, the Supreme Court, or the Presidency. According to the Report Card of American Education, Georgia's overall educational grade is a "B," while Nebraska's grade is a "D." Same country, different states, different educational systems, which means we are taught differently; therefore, we learn differently.

Slavery, Jim Crow, Trail of Tears, Civil Rights, Voting, Vietnam, the Civil War, was there ever an era that "United" us? Even World War II separated Japanese Americans from their birthright and citizenship.

Every experiment has an end result: A discovery. A conclusion. The American experiment; inconclusive.

Dream Time

I think we've all heard that famous quote, "The things dreams are made of." Exactly what are dreams made of? Scientists state that dreams are a manifestation of the conscious mind expressing itself on the subconscious level. In other words, things that are stuck in your head. Or access to memories you stored somewhere in that globe of yours.

I have a different theory. I believe that dreams are a gateway to time travel! Now, before you call the guys in the white van with the straight-jacket hear me out.

Have you ever had a dream, where an event was about to happen. For example, was someone in your dream about to touch your shoulder or grab your arm? Then in the waking world, it was your mother or someone waking you up from your sleep. You predicted the touching in your dream before it happened. Or you dreamed that something was going to fall on your foot. You saw it coming in your dream. Then suddenly, you get a cramp in your toe that wakes you up. For that brief moment, you went back in time in your dream to predict a certain future.

We have dreams of being with our long-lost friends and loved ones in places from the past. We go back in time to when we played kickball in the street or visited that old job we left years ago. Sometimes we alter the dreaming past with fantasies and images, wishing they were there in the waking world. Hell, I remember "stepping" with the Jackson 5 on my front lawn. We changed the group name to the Jackson 6! What about people who predict plane crashes and other accidents in their dreams? Or those who recall images and people years later to solve crimes? What's funny about it all, is the side-effect. Like any good sci-fi movie, memory loss is the side-effect of time travel. I guess that's why we can't remember most of our dreams.

What are dreams made of? Who really knows? Maybe it's that spiritual realm religious groups talk about? Or perhaps it's that 5th dimension where other beings exist? Maybe it's just our brains switching to a different gear? Whatever it is, don't lose sleep over it.

Love Long

How long will you live? How long will you be loved? If you live to be one hundred years old, your life span has been defined. But how long will you be loved by the ones still here? Time transforms the love you have for someone you once loved while they were alive. Think about it! We tend to use "had" instead of "do" when we speak about someone we love, who passed away decades ago.

I had a conversation with a family member about our grandmother. My grandmother raised me at an early age and I considered her the first woman I ever loved.   She passed away in 1992. During our conversation, I noticed I said, I loved Grandma, instead of, I love Grandma. I began to realize the love I have for her transformed to a different level or maybe a different section in my heart. Is it because I no longer can express it to her in person or has time transformed the love into something else? If a love one passes away today, you will still love them as you did yesterday. What causes that love to be different twenty years from now? The absence? Must we continue to have the live contact with others to maintain the current love we feel for one? Or does a new love coat the feelings we once had?

I still love vanilla ice cream because I can still obtain it. I don't love jogging anymore because I can no longer run the distance. Is there a connection or disconnect between now and then? Of course there are different types of love, even with the same people. You love your child differently at six months old versus them at thirty years old. Has love transformed?

Will you still be loved the same if you were one hundred? Would you still love others if you were one hundred? We read about our heroes from the pass. Do we love the person or what the person accomplished? How many times will you listen to that song you love before you get sick of it? From the religious perspective, people love an unseen God. And there are those who love fictional characters such as Mickey Mouse. Yet, have a real mouse in your house and see what happens. Love is a funny thing. I guess it's something we all must figure out in our own way.

Antichrist

It doesn't matter what religion you believe or practice. That's if you believe or practice at all. But one thing's for sure: we've all heard the stories. From the cinematic movies to the sit downs in Sunday school lessons. Evil is coming to slay the world. And that evil is the Antichrist.

According to the eschatology of Christian belief, the Antichrist refers to a person prophesied in the Bible to falsely proclaim himself as a Christ-like savior prior to Jesus Christ's second coming. The question I always ponder over, is whether the Antichrist one person, one people, or one system? Throughout history there has always been one person whose inhumane act can be labeled as demonic. For example, Genghis Khan killed between 20 to 40 million people, which was five to ten percent of the world's population at the time. Was Genghis Khan the Antichrist during that period?

Adolf Hitler ordered the extermination of approximately six million Jewish men, women, and children. According to my grandmother, when the world was at war during WWII, most people in the Western world believe that Hitler was the Antichrist. Was he?

I read on Wikipedia that there was a document released only to Scientology's highest officials stating that the founder of Scientology L. Ron Hubbard, referred to himself as the Antichrist. Only after Hubbard's death did the officials revised the documentation to exclude any reference to Hubbard as the Antichrist.

Parts of 2 John 1:7 in the Bible states, "Most deceivers have gone out into the world…. any such person is the deceiver and the antichrist". Thessalonians 2:3 states, "The Antichrist has been equated with the "man of lawlessness" or "lawless one". Islam calls the Antichrist the al-Dajjal (in Arabic: The Deceiver). The Koran references similar actions and results regarding the last days in the mentioned Bible. Is the Antichrist today's dictator, monarch, or an elected official? Is the Antichrist a person at all?

Maybe the Antichrist is a rotating phenomenon that consists of a person or persons and a specific formula. A mixture of the Seven Deadly Sins (lust, gluttony, greed, sloth, wrath, envy, pride) and the deranged selfishness that created a higher level of hatred and the obsession to control others. For example; the act of slavery is the Antichrist. Massacring an entire people to possess land is the Antichrist. Killing an entire culture because they worship a different deity is the Antichrist. Do people create a formula for hate or does the formula create the people for hate? I'm pretty sure Hitler didn't gather the Jewish people and transport them to the gas chambers of Auschwitz by himself. But hundreds, if not thousands of his followers did. There was a total lack of compassion for human life, even children. Was it the Nazi formula or the individual escorting that five-year-old girl to her death?

I believe no one person can act alone to create such devastation, deceit, and hatred in society. They need others to follow and initiate their wishes. Maybe we humans have been conditioned to accept war when it benefits our way of living? Maybe we have been indoctrinated to believe our specific way of living and thinking should be the standard for others? Why not? It was true back then, and it's true today.

It states in the Bible that man has free will. Will to choose right from wrong. Maybe the Antichrist is that person who amplifies our deep darkest desires within us all? The Book of Revelation spoke of a "beast" coming out of the Earth and the Sea. Is the beast in us, in our hearts, in our desires, during our anger, in our frustration? Do we create the Antichrist due to our free will? To be honest, I just don't know. All I can tell you is that multiple religions with different beliefs have one thing in common: the comings of the last days and the emergence of the Antichrist.

In the words of Bob Marley's Redemption Song lyrics: "Some say it's just a part of it, we've got to fulfill the Book."

Bilingual

We learn multiple languages as a child when both parents are speaking different languages. Or we may learn another language on our own to satisfy a curriculum or to prepare ourselves for that overseas trip. Either way, it opens us up to the cultures where the language is spoken the most.

In Japan, children are taught to speak English in kindergarten as a second language. They continue to learn English through high school as a requirement. It is believed that studying English will boost their ability to thrive in an English-speaking world while maintaining their culture and heritage at the same time.

In Europe, most people learn to speak three to four languages at an early age. Multiple languages are learned due to the geographical proximity of other countries. Most Europeans quickly recognize Americans because we tend to ask the question, "Do you speak English?"   While visiting the Netherlands, I met a young lady working as a cashier in a book store. She thought I was French and began speaking to me in French. When I informed that I was an American tourist, she immediately smiled and started speaking in English. I asked her, "What is the most spoken language in the Netherlands?" She replied, "Dutch, German, French, and English."   I asked her, "What languages do you speak?" She replied, "Dutch, German, French, and English."

The Official Language Act of 1969 made English and French Canada's official government language. Although Nunavut, Inuktitut, and Inuinnaqtun are still spoken by the Indigenous residents. Here in the United States, we tend to forget there are other languages spoken north and south of the border. You would think that each American would be able to speak two to three languages at a minimum. But it is our "better than thou" culture that prohibits the need or will to expand our horizons.

I believe that people who speak multiple languages tend to be more receptive to different cultures. Therefore, reducing prejudice and ignorance, which increases tolerance and understanding.

A Fair-Skinned Story

Most likely there were no fair-skinned Black people in America four hundred years ago. The journey for fair-skinned Blacks began as our ancestral African women were shackled in slave ships and raped at will by their White male slave captors during the Atlantic crossings. The atrocities continued as our Black women were raped by White male slave owners and their compadres. They called us light-skinned Blacks "redbone" back then. Born from violence.

Just imagine, during the time of slavery and Jim Crow in America, no White male rapist or child molester was ever convicted for his horrific crimes against any Black female of any age. It wasn't until May 2, 1959, that four White men were convicted of brutally raping Betty Jean Owens; a Black college student at Florida A&M University in Tallahassee Florida. Each man was sentenced to life in prison, although all of them were paroled, less than nine years later.

Today there are millions of fair-skinned Black Americans. The term "multiracial" is the more accepted wording than "redbone". However, to this day, fair-skinned Black Americans cannot escape scrutiny. I am a fair-skinned Black man, and I can't count the number of times someone has approached me and asked the question; "What are you?" or "What are you mixed with?". Not realizing their curiosity is insulting.

When you think about it, fair-skinned Blacks were among the first Blacks born in America due to the barbaric raping on the slave ships. Yet, for years, many of us were not accepted by the White race or Black race, because our skin color wasn't considered pure by either group. This is just one of the many fair-skinned stories.

Like

I was watching Judge Judy the other day. There were two siblings, one as the plaintiff and the other as the defendant. They both had a different view on what constitutes as to what a loan is, verses what a gift should be? The exchange was a "no-holds-bar" put your family's dirty laundry in the street kind of hearing. After the hearing was concluded, the two siblings were interviewed by the Narrator in the lobby. They both expressed their dislike for each other. Saying things like; I'll never do this again, she can't be trusted, she's a liar, I don't want nothing to do with her. But they both said something similar, "I still love her because she's family, but I don't want anything to do with her ever again."

The statement made me contemplate that "like" is stronger than "love." Do we use family as an excuse for love, even if you don't like the person? There are family members we don't care to have around us, yet when they come-a-coming, we smile and welcome they into our home. After a couple of days, we can't wait for them to jump on the wagon train and head on out. Think about it? We no longer "like" their company.

There are different reasons why couples get divorced. I believe whatever the circumstances, it starts with not liking what a person does or who they become. You rarely hear a person say, "I really like you but I'm divorcing you anyway." How many times have we heard a divorcee say, "I don't want anything to happen to her or him because I still love her or him and the kids." Yet, you won't hear the words, "I still like her or him." Like is stronger than love?

Do you like a friend that you haven't seen in ten years? Or do you love a friend you haven't seen in ten years? Was it love at first sight? Or like at first sight? Do you like going to the movies? Or do you love going to the movies?

Maybe love is just a word we use to substitute for like. Can there be love without like? Can there be like without love?

P.S. I like this!

Happy Help Hurt

"Happy" and "help" don't always go hand in hand. As a father, my views vary from my wife. It's no secret that some mothers are more nurturing than some dads. However, I find that a mother's nurturing manifests from the belief that their actions will lead to the child's immediate happiness. A father's thinking is to "help" the child as a learning experience rather if it leads to immediate happiness or not. Knowing that happiness in the future from lessons learned today is greater than happiness in the present as it is given. Both theories are correct, but the question remains, which one leans more towards "hurt."

Whether we want to admit it or not, "hurt" is the foundation. Hurt can be viewed as a physical or mental pain, a problem to be solved, or an undesirable issue. No matter what we do, "hurt" will find its way into your life. Hurt has a way of sneaking up on us all. Hurt has a way of knocking you down. How will you get back up? Is it "happy" or "help" that reaches out and lifts you up? Is it "happy" or "help" that prepares your child for the many trials ahead?

I believe that "happy" is random. It doesn't follow any pattern, plan, or structure. It can be found anywhere by anyone at any time. That's what makes "happy" the most nurturing aspect to the soul. However, "happy" doesn't solve problems. In some cases, when a person is "hurt", they need to seek "help" to find happiness again. "Help" is logical, tangible, and long-term. "Help" is reason, which doesn't rely on "happy." "Help" is the one who reaches out with the "helping hand." If someone said, "I'll give you a happy hand." You probably say to yourself, "What's that all about?"

Happy, help, and hurt: Can one exist without the other? We try our best to help, to make one happy, so no one would be hurt. I find that every aspect of our lives is intertwined in this paradox.

I Cried a Lot

I cried a lot in the last twenty years

With the death of family and friends

I cried less in the last ten years

I've had more losses than wins

I cried once in the last two years

My youth has slipped away

I didn't cry at all in the last year

But there's more to say

I laughed a lot in the last forty years

Wife, home, and the birth of a boy

It doesn't matter if you cry

When it's tears of joy

The Belief System

During the family Easter get together at my home, one of the traditions we exercised is gathering in a circle, holding hands, and saying a prayer to bless the food. We sometimes take turns saying prayer, but it seems like there's a long pause when asked, "Who wants to give the blessing?" My niece said, "Uncle, you say the prayer." I replied, "Sure, but keep in mind, people have different beliefs, so I won't say anything specific to anyone's belief." As everyone held hands and bowed their heads, I said, "Amen." My sister-in-law who was standing to the left of me, viciously struck my shoulder chest area then immediately apologized as if she had no control of her actions.

I believe people are controlled by the "Belief System." And when that system is challenged, people tend to react one of two ways: Treat it like a teachable moment or treat it like a threat. The Belief System, regardless of your religion creates a practice. That practice over time, becomes a tradition. And as time goes forward, that tradition circles around and becomes the religion.

I've heard people say, "We bless the food to give thanks and nourishment to our body." I've heard, "We pray over the food to ensure purity against things that will harm the body." The amazing thing about it, I never heard or saw anyone bless a stick of chewing gum, a glass of wine, a bottle of water, popcorn at the movies, a candy bar, cough syrup, or any medication. Yet, all these items are consumed through the mouth just like any Easter, Thanksgiving, or Christmas dinner.

Why are there so many physical ways to pray? One word: tradition. Some people stand up with their arms in the air. Others drop to their knees with their head on the floor. Some open their hands with palms up, while others place their hand together as if they're in bondage. And the funny thing about it, is that those who practice their own tradition believe that the others are wrong.

There are mega-churches that can hold thousands of parishioners. There are multi-millionaire Preachers with private jets. Unfortunately, those so-called "Men of God" have preyed on the innocent to satisfy their own sexual sickness. Those people are the masters of the Belief System.

I want to make it clear that your belief in God has nothing to do with the Belief System. The Belief System is a practice which encourages one to behave and think in a certain way. If you believe in God, does it matter what day you go to church? Does it matter what type of food you eat? Does it matter what type of clothes you wear? Does it matter how you pray? I believe the Belief System initials "B.S." just might stand for something else.

The Ten Commandments

For centuries we heard the story of Moses climbing Mount Sinai to receive the Ten Commandments. What if Moses saw the burning bush and was told he would be transported to the year 2024? There he would be given the Ten Commandments which reflect the "don'ts" for this period. Let's imagine what they would be.

1. Thou shall not hack another's bank account on the internet.
2. Thou shall not park in your neighbor's parking space.
3. Thou shall not text or talk on your cell phone while eating dinner in a restaurant.
4. Thou shall not call in sick to work on Friday just because you want a three-day weekend.
5. Thou shall not eat a cheeseburger and fries, and then order a diet soda.
6. Thou shall not drive to a gas station, turn your engine off, and leave your hip-hop gangster rap music blasting so everyone can hear it.
7. Thou shall not conduct a transaction at an ATM machine that takes more than two minutes while someone else is behind you waiting.
8. Thou shall not loan money to relatives who say, "I'll pay you back when I get my income taxes next month."
9. Thou shall not go into a bookstore, pick out a book, sit there and read it for three hours, come back for the next five days, finish the book, and never pay for it.
10. Thou shall not leave one swallow of milk in the container when someone really wanted to eat cereal that morning.

Trust

Who do you trust? Who do you trust to make the decision to pull the plug? Who do you trust to keep that secret? Who do you trust to hold your one hundred-million-dollar lottery ticket? Who do you trust to drive your brand-new car? Who do you trust to have the keys to your house? Who do you trust with your credit card? Who do you trust with your passwords? Who do you trust?

When I was a younger man with no family of my own, I named my mother as my medical proxy as I entered the military. Fast forward thirty years and that decision has changed. Not because of any legal ramifications, but I believe my mother's state of mind at her late age is different. As I view my relationships with my family members, I'm beginning to understand that individual trust plays a major role regarding medical and financial proxies, wills, and having access to other moneys and property. Also, outside influences that can alter the trustee's decision.

When trust is lost, can it be gained again? I guess it depends on which trust was broken. Was it the trust that someone would pay you back for moneys borrowed? Or was it the trust of the heart? Was the broken trust from someone you don't see often? Or from someone you see every day?

In 2012, actor Jackie Chan decided to donate his entire 400-million-dollar fortune to charity because he doesn't trust his son who's been in trouble with the law nor his estranged daughter. Microsoft founder Bill Gates announced in 2016 that he would donate most of his fortune to charity instead of leaving it to his children, saying it would, "distort their view of the world". Is this because he doesn't trust their life decisions with so much money?

As I get older, my views on trust has changed. Because I realize the people, I know views on trust has also changed as well. Some views have changed for the better, some for the worse, and some remained the same. Trust has become a fragile thing. It's not easily given to anyone and it's not easily earned either. I guess the only way to gain trust from someone, is to trust yourself first.

Money and Justice

It makes me angry when I hear about someone committing a crime which carries a substantial number of years in prison. Then suddenly, their prison time is reduced because of a plea-bargain. The courts decides the cost and time to prosecute the case isn't feasible, therefore the criminal act receive leniency versus the same criminal act that doesn't take a plea-bargain. Roughly 90% of all criminal cases in the United States is settle by the plea-bargain rather than a jury trial. Whatever happen to "being judged by your peers"? Is this action the result of "money over justice"?

Is the "money over justice" the only way to rectify the problem? I'm not saying it's completely wrong, because there are those who need to be made whole. But, when you take a closer look at things, it's all about the money?

How many times have we heard a person settling out of court with a disclosed amount. Money over justice, or justice rectified by money?

Recently the Justice Department award the U.S. Female Gymnastic team $130,000,000 for the FBI's incompetence regarding the handling of the sexual assaults reported to them. Although their coach is serving life in prison, no amount of money can undo what happen to these young women. Is this an example of justice and money working together to rectified a problem?

I once heard a guy purposely committed a crime, so he could go to prison for five years. After his five-year term, he stated; in prison he was able to complete his bachelors and master's degree. Have free dental and health care. Free housing with free meals. He said, "a person who completed a four-year college may not be locked up in jail, but they are in prison due to massive student loans and trying to make a living. Where's the justice in that."

The Great Separator

Are you aware of the enemies of mankind? The weapons we created to eliminate our existence. From the bow and arrows of times long ago to the massive nuclear arsenal that can destroy the world a thousand times over. There is one weapon used throughout the centuries. One weapon used to perfection. There is one weapon that's more powerful than them all: Religion.

Religion has been mankind's true nemesis since the recording of history. Cultures, languages, civilizations, the innocent, and knowledge have been destroyed in the name of religion. Religion does not promote fellowship outside its own entrenched belief, because it acts as the "Great Separator." Even within its own religious sect, there is separation in the religion itself. For example; within Christianity there are Lutheran, Baptist, Methodist, Presbyterian, Roman Catholic, and more. Within Islam there are Sunni, Shi'a, Sufism, and Ibadi. Within Sikhism there are Namdharis, Nirankari, Nirmala, and Radha Swami. And let's not forget the Jewish sect; Reform Judaism, Orthodox, Conservative, and Hasidic.

The United States has created three new religions. It's called Democrats, Republicans, and MAGA Republicans. It might be politics, but they all share the same ideology as any religion, if you don't believe in the way they think, you are an outsider, you're wrong and they're right. Even if you decide not to be part of "these" religions, you are viewed as "less than," different, or ignorant, because you're not one of them.

Not all is lost. When a person discover spirituality over religion, that person embraces fellowship, not separation. Fellowship without conditions. Fellowship with no intentions.

Singer John Lennon said, "Imagine there's no countries, it isn't hard to do. Nothing to kill or die for, and no religion too."

I would add, "Give love and kindness, should be the least. Because religion has shown it doesn't want peace."

Antisemitism

It's no secret the Jewish people have been persecuted through the ages. From the ancient biblical days to the Nazi concentration camps. We use the word antisemitism to describe the hostility and discrimination against Jews as a religious, ethnic, or racial group. But the question I have is, why don't we use singular definitions to describe atrocities towards other ethnic groups or religions?

During the period of the Mongol Empire from 1206 to 1227. Genghis Khan ruled with an iron fist. He led a military campaign across China and Central Asia that killed an estimated 40 million people. Yet, there isn't a singular word used to describe the hostility and killing of people of Asian descent.

There were over 54,000 voyages during the Transatlantic Slave Trade. The slave trade was a global event, transporting enslaved Africans to North America, South America, Europe, and parts of the Middle East. Slavery resulted in a vast number of men, women, and children dying during capture, transport, and enslavement. The true number is unknown, but the loss of life is estimated to be as low as 2 million to as high as 60 million. Which doesn't account for the centuries of lynchings. And yet, there is no singular word used to describe the hostility and killing of people of African descent.

The Gnadenhutten Massacre, the Sand Creek Massacre, the Mankato Executions, the Trail of Tears, forced removal, just to name a few. These are some of the horrors and atrocities the Indigenous people had to endure. During the Pre-Columbian period (Christopher Columbus) there was an estimated 50-100 million Indians on this continent. According to the 2020 U.S. Census, that number is 3.7 million, which also includes Alaska. Where is that singular word to describe this?

Evil Heritage

A Virginia school district approved to reinstate two Confederate names on their schools: Stonewall Jackson High School and Ashby-Lee Elementary School. Some residents argued that restoring those names would restore their heritage. The Shenandoah County School District voted 5-1 to reinstate the names. Apparently, members of the school board didn't study the Confederacy's goals for Black people in America.

There are so many angles I can take regarding this decision. I'll start with this: The school district did not consider how Black students would feel to have his or her diploma with the words Stonewall Jackson or Ashby-Lee displayed in the family's home as a symbol of achievement. Knowing that if Jackson, Ashby, and Lee had been successful in their campaigns, no Blacks would have ever been allowed to attend school in the first place.

It's so incomprehensible for people who embrace the Confederacy by saying, "It's my heritage." Because they never explain what the heritage is. They never say or point out how their "heritage" contributed to the positive growth of this country for all races. They never talk about the atrocities committed by their "heritage." They never talk about how their "heritage" traded, sold, and separated Black families because they were considered property. Or how lives were destroyed based on the color of their skin. Their heritage is women, men, and children of color being molested and raped with no consequences for the White male rapist. Black mothers having to work the cotton fields one day after given birth. Black men and young Black boys being lynched. Black men, women, and children being mutilated, whipped, drowned, burned, starved, and chained. This is their heritage.

Hitler and the Third Reich declared war on the citizens of Germany, and in return, modern Germany will always consider the Nazis the enemy of the state. After World War II, Germany destroyed all symbols and statues of Nazi Germany. In the United States, all elected and non-elected persons serving the people must take the Oath of Allegiance before serving. Within the Oath, is the statement, "I will support and defend the Constitution and laws of the United States of America against all enemies, foreign and domestic."

The Confederacy did not support or defend the Constitution and laws of the United States. The Confederacy fought and still fights for their statues and symbols to be a mainstay in this country. The Confederacy fought against the United States. The Confederacy killed soldiers defending the United States. The Confederacy was the domestic enemy. So, why are the Shenandoah County School District members naming schools after the Confederacy Third Reich?

Who are those five members? And what Oath of Allegiance do they pledge to?   What heritage do they embrace?

Music Talks

Humans create music, but what exactly is music, and who does it speak to? Does music speak to the soul or the soul of a generation? Throughout the world, music in some countries reflects the culture of the people. American Indians danced around the fire at the beat of the drums. Those same drum beats, sent messages of oncoming threats to the village. The Civil War trumpets sounded the signal to charge into battle or fall back in retreat.

What causes music to transform through the decades? We quickly recognize the Rag-Tag sounds from the 1920s and 1930s versus Rock-n-Roll from the 1950s. The 1960s Motown sound was totally different from the pop-soul mix Top 100 hits from the 1980s. Let's not forget disco.

How does an artist know that a new genre is being created when no example exists?

I believe music speaks for that particular generation at the time of its creation. Our teenagers today don't relate to music outside their generation, because their generation experiences a different environment. The same is said for someone over 80 years old listening to Dr. Dre and NWA. It doesn't speak to them.

When you think of the 1960s, what comes to mind is the Vietnam War, Civil Rights, civil unrest, liberation, and assassinations. Marvin Gaye's, "What's Going On," The Who, Jimmie Hendrix, and Woodstock. They all seem to go together. A generational connection. This doesn't mean that different music isn't enjoyed by all generations.

I believe music is an aurora that resonated from our existence that is capture in sound. Something we dance to, sometimes cry to, sounds that calm us, lyrics that inspire us, and beats that enrage us.

But let's not forget classical music. It's hundreds of years old and yet, it's still listened to today. Maybe it speaks to us better, because there are no words.

Stay Strong

We are strong. We can strive for peace and be strong. We can advocate self-reliance and awareness, and be strong. We can elevate our culture, our race, our heritage, and be strong. We can remain true to ourselves and be strong.

We are attacked because we are educated. We are attacked because we are loved. We are attacked because we are respected. We are attacked because we don't conform to the "colonizer's" demands, to the colonizer's fears. We are attacked because we are strong.

We are called militants, heathens, anti-American, bastards, and niggas. Yet, we are strong. We are called troublemakers, communists, and weak. Yet, we are strong. We've been ridiculed, beaten, assassinated, and murdered. Yet, we remain and always will be strong.

Annoying

Sometimes, you just don't want to be bothered! Every time you try to take an afternoon nap, the phone rings.

Sometimes, you want to drive fifty miles an hour on the highway. And there's always someone behind you honking the horn, trying to speed you up. What about that person in the grocery store express line with eighty-five items? Are you "f-ing" kidding me! Let's not forget the twenty-five insurance, injury lawyers, and medication commercials during that thirty-minute TV show you're watching.

Older folks always talk about simpler times, because there weren't as many things to annoy them. Think about it. Let's compare the year 1924 to 2024. In 1924, there probably wasn't any road rage because there wasn't as many cars on the road. That's if there was a road to drive on. In 2024, there are so many cars, you may not be able to even get on the road. And road rage; good luck, drive at your own risk. In 1924, people paid attention when walking on the sidewalk or in a store. In 2024, people are talking and texting on their cell phones with their heads down. They tend to bump into you without an "excuse me" or "oh, I'm sorry." In 1924, a Gentleman would lay his coat down so the lady wouldn't have to walk in the puddle. In 2024, you must be out of your damn mind if you think a guy is going to put his London Fog cashmere trench coat in the mud, then have someone step on it? Not in "this" lifetime!

Now, of course 1924 versus 2024 was much worse for Black Americans because of the Jim Crow Laws and all the other racism in America. But here are some facts to ponder over. In 1924, only 4% of all Black children were born out of wedlock. In 2024, that number is 43%. In 1924, Black Americans were outpacing White Americans in economic growth. Now, in 2024, the wealth gap has grown further apart with 29% of Black Americans as homeowners versus 73% of White Americans. Even worse, the median wealth for a Black family is $46,600 versus a White family is $74,919, according to the Urban League 2024 State of Black America Report. Now that's annoying.

Mammy Two Shoes

I'm going to say something that a fair amount of people think, but they won't say out loud. Some of those Tom and Jerry racist cartoons back in the day were really funny!

Remember Mammy Two Shoes? She was the stereotypical heavy-set Black female maid with saggy socks that lived with Tom and Jerry. You only saw her from the neck down. She spoke with a stereotypical low-educated southern vocabulary.

As a child, I would laugh so hard when Mammy Two Shoes would chase Tom around the house with a broom. Saying things like, "I is the boss" and "if you break thangs, yuzu going out...O.W.T., out." And, as a young child in the 1960's, I wasn't aware or even knowledgeable of deliberate stereotyping I was being fed.

The original Tom and Jerry theatrical ran from 1940 to 1958. Decades later, there were three newer versions that introduced new maids and homeowners. The first was a Black woman with proper grammar and nicer clothing. The second was a thin, white teenager. And the third was a heavy-set White maid. None of the three really caught on, so the studios decided to run the cartoon without them.

I recall my mother watching the Little Rascals with Buckwheat and Stymie. Stereotype or not, all I know, this was the only time I saw my mother crying because she was laughing so hard.

Stereotype images should always be challenged. But sometimes things are just funny. Do we accept stereotypes if they make us laugh? If you go to a comedy show like Chris Rock, Wanda Sykes, or Dave Chappelle, part of the entertainment is making fun of stereotypes. It doesn't mean you're going to leave the show as a converted racist.

I enjoyed Mammy Two Shoes. She made me laugh, and she brought a little happiness to my heart. Even today, I would search YouTube and watch Mammy chase Tom with a smile on my face and giggles in my belly.

No Little Lie

We encourage our kids to be honest. To tell the truth, even if it makes them feel uncomfortable. The truth is always the right thing to do. This all sounds noble, but parents and adults lie to their kids and others all the time. Yet, we expect our children to carry the banner of honesty. Does it affect us all in the long run? Maybe or maybe not. All I know is we all lie.

Santa Claus.

The tooth fairy.

Officer, I wasn't speeding, I was going 55.

You can be anything you want to be.

Sorry, he's not here. May I take a message.

I'll be there in a minute.

I'm sorry, this seat is taken.

I got a headache.

We should get together again.

I was over a friend's house.

Oh, it was a wrong number.

It's not your fault.

I'm busy right now.

We should just be friends.

What are you thinking about? Nothing.

Sure, we had a good time.

Yeah, it tastes pretty good.

They lived happily ever after.

Dinosaurs

I went to retrieve my mail the other day. To my surprise in the mailbox was the Yellow Pages phone book. It wasn't as thick as the Yellow Pages in the past. Nevertheless, there it was, one of the original dinosaurs. As I looked at the nostalgic relic, I wondered what other dinosaurs are still out there and where would I find them?

I ventured to the nearest Walmart Superstore in search of these prehistoric items. It was a daunting task, but I managed to dig up these once-used fossils.

A portable AM/FM radio: I'll give anyone $10 if you can show me a teenager walking around with a portable radio. And speaking of walking, I actually saw a Walkman. It had to be digitized, because there are no cassette tapes anymore.

Disposable cameras: Just about everyone today utilizes their cell phone as the camera of choice. Now I can tell you, my mother still uses those things. By the way, my mother is 86 years old.

Keychain flashlights: it looks good attached to your keyring, but it was never used for what it was intended. It was never practical to put your key in the door lock and shine the light from your keychain at the same time. There's now a flashlight on the cell phone.

Archie comic books next to the checkout line: in the 1970s Archie, Reggie, Veronica, Betty, and Jughead were the thing. Fast forward to 2024, and it's all about the online challenges: Anime, Dragon Ball Z, Tour of Duty, Warcraft, and the Teenage Mutant Ninja Turtles.

Oh my god! Lo and behold, a wall phone with the six-foot cord.

It was fun digging up these old fossils. But the largest fossil of all, the king of the dinosaurs, the Tyrannosaurus Rex: the paper map.

I don't know anyone who still utilizes a large city or state map for directions. I recall my grandfather having about 50 maps inside his 1951 Ford. Whenever he would travel beyond South Carolina, he would grab a map, spread it out over the hood of his car, and talk about the direction he would take.

The king of directions today is called GPS. And it doesn't stand for "good 'ole prehistoric stuff."

Aware of Nothing

A few years ago, I was scheduled a routine colonoscopy. The medical nurse administered anesthesia and asked me to count from one hundred backwards. I think I made it to ninety-five before I completely passed out. And when I meant completely out; I mean out of reality, out of dreams, out of existence. Nothing existed; no thoughts of the past, present, or future. Not even time itself was immune to the "nothingness."

The experience greatly changed my prospective on life and death itself. I realized that "nothingness" is an absence of awareness. Everything we experience in life, everything we believe is a result of awareness. I would ponder; without awareness, nothing can be created from the human mind.

In the story of Adam and Eve. As a result of their indiscretion, they became "aware" of their nakedness when consuming the fruit from the tree of knowledge. The smarter we become as humans, the more we are aware. This theory would explain why humans continue to create and invent new things. Awareness equals knowledge.

Every human whom ever existed have two things in common: (1) You are born and (2) therefore you will die. Religions teaches us that there will be an "awareness" after death. That awareness will exist in a place of paradise or in a place of torment. Nothingness is not a place after death. Nothingness is not a journey. With nothingness neither pain nor happiness exist. Nothingness is nothingness.

I was once asked, "Are you afraid to die?" I replied, "No, because I'm absolutely sure one or two things are going to happen…something or nothing. So why be afraid about something that will eventually happen to us all."

I guess the word "nothingness" doesn't sound poetic carved on a headstone. But when you think about it, it's no different from Rest in Peace.

Just a Minute

Human life is just a blink of the eye, compared to the existence of the universe. So, what if we looked at life years in terms of minutes?   If a year was a minute, what time will it be in your life?

From the first slave brought to North American to the first Black President took 6 hours and 30 minutes (1619-2008).

From Galileo being persecuted by the Catholic Church for proving that planets orbits the Sun, to Neil Armstrong walking on the Moon took exactly 6 hours (1609-1969).

From the Renaissance period when overweight women was considered beautiful compared to today's so-called size one Super Models. 11 hours and 40 minutes (14th century- 2010).

From riding a horse in the wild west to driving a 500 horse power pony in the wild west; the Mustang GT.   2 hours (Early 19th century to today)

From the Rag-Time jams at the back wood mosquito infested Juke Joint, to the Gangster-Rap blasting from the low rider. 1 hour (1920's-1980's).

Dr. Martin Luther King, Malcolm X, Cleopatra, Fats Waller, Anna Nicole Smith, Stonewall Jackson, Wild Bill Hickok, and Junior Parker all lived only 39 seconds.

You only work 30-40 seconds before you retire from the job.   Your kids live with you for less than 21 seconds; if you're lucky. That car payment of yours is 5 to 7 seconds. And it takes you less than 17 seconds to go from kindergarten to completing a Master's degree. When you look at it, things go pretty quick.

Unfortunately, I hate to say. There isn't a time clock small enough to measure your sex life.

Talk Away

I went to the gym is morning around 10:30 am. I usually work out with my son, after he gets off work at 2:00 pm or I go early in the morning at 5:00 am. The 10:30 am gym members are mostly of the retirement crowd. Those who are no longer tided to a work schedule.

One thing I encounter the most, is people wanting to talk to you while you are trying to work out. As I started to work my abs, this guy came up to me and just started talking out of the blue. He was saying things like, "These young are so f-ing rude," "You're old enough to understand?", "You and I beat our kids in the 80's, those were the good days", "Most men are Republicans", and on and on and on. I couldn't get this guy to shut up! I tried to end the conversation without being rude to no avail. I realized if a person is not experienced in how to end a conversation, they may appear as rude.

I've taking multiple communication classes in college, I've been on job interview boards, and counseled employees regarding employment issues. And all that time, I don't ever remember learning on how to master ending a conversation. We are accustomed to saying good-bye, see you later, or let's stay in touch. When inside of us, we're really thinking, "will you just go away."

I guess the "master of good-byes" also depend who you are communicating with. Before I speak on the phone with my mother, I always have my wife around to hand her the phone. I would say to my mom, "Well, here's Jackie, she wants to say hi to you." Never to be handed the phone again.

I guess the key is to have a rehearsed line for specific people. Too bad some of the famous endings like, "Amen" and "The End" doesn't work on individuals. Maybe to end a conversation we have to say something most adults are familiar with: That'll be twenty dollars please!

Trapped

Are you trapped in a relationship that continues to turn conversations into arguments? Happiness into heartache? Warm feelings to chill isolation? Are you trapped in a house you no longer call home? Where the hot meals taste cold and the atmosphere is always hot.

Are you trapped in a job where they don't respect your opinion, your hard work, your dedication, or you? Raise? What raise?

Are you trapped in a neighborhood where crime is Christmas every day for the crook? Reflections of "The Purge" when the Sun goes down? Metal bars on every window and doors.

Are you trapped in an education system that caters to politics before education? Altered history, no trade skills? Aged out of eighth grade with a third-grade reading level. Welcome to high school.

Mr. Time is your captor and Ms. Hope locks you in that cage. Mr. Time doesn't care how long you remain trapped because he has all the time in the world. Ms. Hope is the illusion; dreams of someday you will escape the cage. The only ones that can help you are Ms. Courage and Mr. Action.

Ms. Courage will empower your spirit to rise up. Ms. Courage tells you that there is something better. Ms. Courage emphasizes that fear of change is not a bad thing. Stand tall, stand firm, look your captors in the eyes, and say, you're not going to take it anymore. Ms. Courage teaches you, not to be afraid.

Mr. Action unlocks the cage. Mr. Action doesn't tolerate the abuse to the soul. Mr. Action moves to a better place, asks for that raise, works hard to get that promotion, or utilizes his skills somewhere else. Mr. Action studies and reads material outside of the structured norm. Mr. Action refuses to settle. Mr. Action will not hesitate to learn something new to better himself.

With Ms. Courage and Mr. Action on your side, you will be free from the cage. You will be trapped, no longer.

Labels

What are you? What banner do you carry? What do you want people to see you as? There are labels placed upon us by others. There are labels we happily choose by choice.

One person can be an Irish-American, a Christian, a New Yorker, a Republican, and a Red Socks fan all at the same time. There are labels of our choosing, at which we can change at any time. Then there are labels placed upon us not by our choosing, rather by what we do or what we did. Such as; doctor, teacher, writer, thief, con-man, cheater, parents, terrorist, just to name a few. These labels are given to us based on our actions. Some actions are for the good of mankind others are not.

One disturbing thing about labels, is they all come with assumptions. People assume that a person behaves or think a certain way because their "label" is different. I once had a person say to me, "You don't act like a Christian!" That person expected a certain behavior because I carried the label once. I heard my sister said to my other sister, "You don't act Black!" Is there a certain way to act if you carry the Black label?

Labels have always been with us since the beginning of time. Good versus evil, civilized versus savage. And I believe the we will continue to use them to define those who share our belief and those who do not. Maybe we need labels as part of our existence? Without it, there would be no verbal distinction to identify a person role or belief. Who knows?

All I know, all my life I've been label many things. Some I was happy with and others I was not. But it doesn't matter who you are, where you live, what you do, or what you did, we all will have one label in common without assumptions: Deceased.

Hey Big Mouth

When people are asked, what is the most important organ or part of the body? Most folks would reply; the heart, the brain, or the lungs as a general answer. You never heard anyone say the mouth.

Most body parts have one function. Some can even be replaced such as a lung, liver, or kidney when it's no longer functioning properly. I believe the mouth is the most important and most multifunctional area of the body. Here are several functions related to the mouth.

1. You cannot survive without eating and drinking. The mouth is the tunnel for all nutrition.
2. When your body rejects that undesirable digestive substance, you mouth is the exit point for vomit.
3. You can squirt water with your mouth.
4. You can shoot spitballs with a straw.
5. You mouth is used for breathing when your nostrils are clogged or for breathing when scuba diving.
6. It's also used for blowing out that birthday candle or blowing up balloons.
7. You can give life back with CPR with your mouth.
8. You show love and compassion with a kiss with those lips on your mouth.
9. You give oral sex with that mouth of yours.
10. You make multiple impressions with your mouth.
11. You can sing and speak multiple languages with your mouth.
12. You can hold objects.
13. You can paint a portrait with your mouth.
14. You can make music by whistling.

My favorite is, you can smile and make someone's day with your mouth.

The Bail Out

When Barack Obama was elected President, one of the first executive orders implemented was the banking and auto industry bail out. Money was giving to General Motors, Chrysler, and numerous banks to save jobs and retirement savings. As parents we bail out our children when they lose their jobs, pay an unexpected bill, or fall on hard times.

The Republican Congress argued the auto industry and banks should not be bailed out. That it was not the responsibility of government to give money to private industries. The Obama Administration argued that certain industries were just too big to fail. And that failure would cause a catastrophic effect on the economy and individual retirements.

As parents the parallel argument within us is the same. On one hand, we want our children to stand on their own. To be responsible for the decisions they make, and to learn from those decisions regardless if it leads to despair.   On the other hand, we want to assist in the struggles they encounter in life. We know how it feels, we know the pain it can cause, and we know the path of despair. So, like the Obama Administration we issue a bail out.

What's the big difference between an Executive Administration and the so-call Parent Administration? Actually nothing! Both administrations can choose to continue to distribute funds regardless on the push back from outside voices. Both administrations want the industry or child to learn and make adjustments to avoid future failures. Both administrations usually doesn't place a time frame on funds to be paid back. And both administrations rely on good faith from the borrowers to return moneys given.

I believe the bail outs are a good thing. The industries that thrive from the bail outs tend to pay the more taxes to the government and employ more people that contributes to the economy. As for our children, we hope the bail out teaches them a life lesson and hopefully bail us out when we are unable to take care of ourself physically, mentally, and financially.

The Contract

"Til death do us part," this is the terms of the contract. A promise you verbally agreed to obey on that commemorating day. The contract maybe different, based on time and tradition. But, at the end of the day, it's all the same.

From ancient Egypt to the far away islands in the Pacific, there was marriage. From the Odin worshipping Vikings to the Sun worshipping Inkas, there was marriage. Marriage is the only commonality that all mankind share without the knowledge of other civilizations.

The first stage of the contract starts with the ceremony: Jumping the broom, wearing crowns, breaking a bell, the white tsunokakushi, even marrying a tree first. This stage follows with the rice throw, gathering of the feast, celebratory dance, and eventually the copulating that cements the couple. Whatever the first stage tradition might be, it leads to the meat of the contract which means existing together. And that's where the fun starts…I'm being sarcastic!

You know what's funny? There are 29 animal species on this planet that mate for life. Animals! They honor their marriage. Yet, humans need a contract and ceremony to consummate their marriage. Hoping that the mating process remains between the two. But the contract is more than the mating commitment. It's the honor system, the cooking class, the daycare, the nightshift, the security guard, the love boat, and fantasy island. It's the "I do," "I will honor" and "Let no man or woman come between you."

Whatever the reason, there are those who honor the contract and those who do not. Humans are complex and yet simple. We are the only species that have desires outside of commitments and survival? Maybe we humans have more in common with the Black Widow.

Once the female Black Widow spider mates with the male spider, she kills him and start to devour him. Some of us, male and female do the same when we devour the contract.

Crossroad

There are many crossroads in life. I'd like to tell you about one of the most significant crossroads that changed my life forever.

From my sophomore year to my senior year in high school, I would spend my afterschool hours at a place called RTP. I believe it stood for Recruitment and Training Program, but I don't quite remember. There were counselors there to help intercity high school students with various things and a place to go after school. I attended the center every day after school for mainly these reasons: One, I really like the counselors and two, I despise going back to my dysfunctional home. If I had a choice, I would have set up a tent inside the center.

The two counselors I connected with most were Linda Pinkard and Kathy Lewis. Kathy was the cool, no-nonsense White girl in the predominately Black neighborhood who didn't take any mess from anyone. She lived in the hood, taught in the hood, and married to Sam (a brother) with that cool 1969 Buick Riviera. I would stay at the center until closing. Kathy and Sam used to drive me home and occasionally invite me to dinner at their house. Kathy's kindness helped restore some faith in people. She taught me that there are people who give from the heart without asking for anything in return.

There's an old saying: There are those who speak a lot and say little. And there are those who say little but speak a lot. Linda was the strong silent type. But when she spoke you listened. The wisdom I gained from her is unmeasurable.

I applied to attend the University of Buffalo in my senior year of high school. I didn't know too much about the application process, considering I would be the first one in my family ever to attend a four-year university. I got no assistance with the application or financial aid paperwork from home or any other family member. So, I set out to complete the process by myself.

Weeks later, I received a letter from the University of Buffalo. It was a Saturday. I must have waited hours before I opened that letter. I opened the letter. It said, I was not accepted at the University. I was devastated; not only because the University of Buffalo was the only school I applied too; I didn't have any other plans to escape the hood.

The following Monday after school, I went to the center. I must have had a look that displayed my disappointment of the news I received that Saturday. Without me saying a word, Linda Pinkard said, "Trent, come to my office." I entered her office, she asked me to close the door and said, "I've never seen this look on your face before, what's going on." As a tear rolled from my eye, without speaking, I reached in my pocket and gave her the letter. She read it and said, "Follow me." We went to her car in the parking lot. She asked me to get in and we drove to the University's admission building. We walked up to the second or third floor. Linda reached in her purse and pulled out a key to one of the office doors. Apparently, it was her office at the University! She typed something at her typewriter, placed it an inter-office mail envelope, then left it on her desk. Whatever she did made a difference, because a week later I received a letter from the University accepting me into the freshman class at the University of Buffalo.

Because of budget cuts, the center closed the following year. I got a chance to visit Linda before it closed and got her number and address. I would write her on occasion to show that I will never forget what she did for me. I would say to her, "You saved my life." She would reply, "No, you did this all on your own."

As time went on, I lost contact with Linda. The last time I had any contact with her, she was a director at a college somewhere in Tennessee. The internet was not invented then, so I really didn't have a way to track her whereabouts unless she continued her correspondence by snail mail. I didn't know her age, but I'm guessing she would probably be in her mid to upper eighties by now.

I've learned that the crossroads of live start with the people you know. Some roads may lead you down a dark place in the tunnel. While others may be the guiding light that leads your way out.

Spiderwebs

I had a conversation with my stepmother earlier this year. She told me of an old remedy the southern folks would utilize back in the day, when they received a cut on their bodies. She told me they would place spiderwebs on the laceration. And miraculously, the wound would heal with no evidence that there was a cut at all. Of course, I didn't quite believe her, but then I heard the same thing from another matriarch in the family, then another, then another. She also named the plants they would use for other illnesses no longer exist because of construction and modernization in parts of the Carolinas.

It kind of makes you wonder: What other home remedies were lost because of modernization, or our elders not passing the knowledge on to the next generation, or the next generation just not listening to those "old folks?"

I remember, as a child, A & D Ointment was the only medicine we had in the house. If you received a cut, bumped your head, had hemorrhoids, a rash, or clogged nostrils; A & D Ointment to the rescue.

I saw a medical documentary where doctors here in the United States were using live maggots, yes, live maggots to heal a patient's severed arm. As a matter of fact, it's one of the oldest ancient therapies that is still used today. It's called, Maggot Therapy.

There are still hundreds of home remedies out there that do the same thing as any over-the-counter medicines. Unfortunately, you'll never learn this in school or by some advertising on television. That's because it's all about the Benjamins.' We are a drugged-up nation, believing that somehow someway we're going to need a product from Pfizer, Merch, Lilly, AbbVie, or Johnson & Johnson. Think about it; half of all the commercials you see on TV are medicine related. Who are the real drug dealers?

The spider no longer owns the web. Because the web no longer catches flies. It's designed to catch you.

Castaways

The Bible tells the story of why Satan and his followers were cast out of heaven and placed on Earth. Maybe that's how the story was explained by the ancient scholars? Or, maybe the real story is how we humans were cast out or separated from a higher intelligent species than our own?

If I was the Creator of human beings, would I place them in an environment not indigenous to their nature? Think about it. The Earth is 71% water, yet we can only drink 3.5% of it. Most of what we consume must be grown or cooked over a fire. No other species on Earth wear clothing to protect themselves from the elements. And we have this bad habit of killing things; Not for consumption, because we fear it, it annoys us, it has something we want, it looks different, it behaves different, or just for sport.

Why do humans have this internal urge to battle? Gladiators fighting to the death in ancient Rome to today's National Football League. Even something simple, like running track or playing chess. Wherever humans reside on this planet throughout time, there has been some kind of battle among tribes, cultures, or nations. Why do we feel good after the battle? After the win. What chromosome in our genetic material forces us to be this way? Did the Creator contaminate the petri dish?

Let's imagine that Heaven is the name of a peaceful planet were all the species live in complete harmony. Then the Creator decided to make a new form of animal called Humans. The Creator decides to release these Humans among the rest of the species. Shortly after, Humans began to fight one another, kill other species, and just make a mess of things. So, the Creator decided to corral all the Humans from Heaven and place them on this planet we call Earth, with instructions on how Humans were intended to act. In those instructions, the Creator said he or she will return to Earth to retrieve those who have learned from those instructions, to ensure Humans will be able to live among the species on planet Heaven again. Until then, we are the castaways, stuck on Gilligan's Island.

The Walk

Some of my Black brothers like the bootylicious booty. Some of my Caucasian brothers like the cleavage in your face chest.   Some of my Asian brothers like the long silky legs. And some of my Latino brothers prefer those street-side curvy hips. Is it love or lust at first sight? Whatever it is, it works.

For me, it's "The Walk." There's a certain walk a woman has that gets my attention. The Walk comes with a sense of confidence and class. It's not that phony walk some women do to make themselves look sexy. Please! Give me a break! Nor is it that firm walk to let all her coworkers know she is the boss. It's that eye catching stride that says her body from head to toe is in perfect harmony. The Walk radiates with a sense of intelligence, kindness, and grace.

I find that The Walk comes with some charming accessories: beautiful eyes, a sense of humor and a gorgeous smile.   I married a woman with The Walk and I never get tired of looking at her stride. I often wondered if she knows that I enjoy looking at her walk every day?

I guess the best advice I can give, if you are a guy who loves The Walk. If you find that special girl with it, try to catch her. Don't walk. Run.

Traditions

We all grow up. We often leave behind family lessons, taught to us in our youth. And there are those who escape the traditions they are expected to inherit.

Meet my friend, Sophia: A brilliant young lady. She works as an accountant at a financial company. Sophia has a tattoo on her left arm and leg. Sophia rides a classic Indian Motorcycle. Sophia has a American Bulldog. Sophia was born and raised in California. Sophia is not traditional. Sophia is an American.

Sophia's parents are practicing Muslims who were born and raised in Afghanistan. They are traditional and steadfast. Do they accept Sophia's lifestyle? Do they accept her lack of traditional inheritance? Does it matter? Is it any different from any child born in America or elsewhere, who decides to venture in a different direction from their parents inherited traditions?

We want our children to be doctors, lawyers, or some profession to ensure they will be financially sound once they leave the nest. Instead, they decide to pursue a degree in Art. We want our children to dress for success, instead they stamp their bodies with tattoos because it's fashionable. We want our children to maintain the same religious beliefs placed upon them in their youth. Instead, they become an Atheist. Is this an example of family traditions lost? Or is this an example of a person becoming a self-aware individual?

Some traditions change and some remain the same. Those who believe that traditions should not change, say it maintains the culture which is the structure for the people. While others who believe it should change, say it's the evolution of an individual. Because without evolution, there's no growth.

The Penny

I have an idea to save the United States money and reduce some of the stress we all experience from time to time. The idea is for the United States Mint to stop making the penny.

Sixty years ago, you were able to buy penny candy with a penny. In today's world, there is absolutely nothing in any store, that you can purchase a penny with. How many times have you seen a dirty penny on the ground and walked right past it? If that was a dirty quarter, you wouldn't hesitate to bend over, pick it up and place it in your pocket. Then tell someone later, you were lucky today because you found a quarter.

The penny is made from copper which is a precious metal that can be utilized in other areas such as smart phones, TVs, and other components. I believe tech companies will reduce the cost of their products if the components to make them were in abundance.

I saw a report that the United States was short of pennies because people were not cashing them in; proves that people love to save pennies which prompts the U.S. Mint to make more.

I also believe people would be more reluctant to toss that quarter in the wishing well rather than the penny. This will certainly save you some moola. I also think the U.S. Mint should stop making nickels and dimes for that same reason.

Imagine our coin currency was only the quarter. Counting change at the store would be much easier. Counting money in your piggy bank would be a breeze. And carrying different coins at the Dollar Store to have exact change won't be necessary.

But there is one thing I would miss: Abraham Lincoln. Conspiracist would say the United States place President Lincoln on the penny to: One, to make his worth less than the other currencies. Two, turn him to a person of color because he freed Blacks that were enslaved. And three, if you noticed, Lincoln is the only President on the coin that face to the right, while the others face to the left. Some believe this was purposely done so it appears that the other Presidents turned their backs on him.

I've always wondered, if George Washington was the first President, then why isn't he number one on the penny, instead of number twenty-five as to the quarter? Could the conspiracist have a point?

What Are You Saying?

I've been told, English as a second language speakers, that our language is confusing. Not because it's spoken English itself, but how we use it. I'll start with this example. The word "saw" means seeing an object in past tense and a tool we use to cut wood.

We use the word cowboy to identify a man with a six- shooter and a horse galloping on the open plains. Yet a cow is a female and the bull is the male. What about the vulgar quote, "Fuck that shit." Are we really having sex with manure?

 When the younger generation make a mistake, they love to say, "My bag." Paper or plastic?

What about, "I'll catch you later." Who exactly is going to throw me at you? Or will I just throw myself off a building? Please don't drop me! Remember when "that's bad" meant it's really good. Or "that's cool" really meant it's hot.

Don't get so angry when someone call you an asshole. From a biological stand point, we all have a little asshole in us, or I should say behind us.

The word fucken or ficken originated from the Old Germanic language meaning sex. Anyone having sex with a mother. Well, you are a mother-fucker.

 One of the most puzzling quotes to me is, "What the hell." "What the hell" is used just like the word "saw." People use it when they are surprised at something, when they don't care about something, or when they are angry about something.

In my case, I'm just confused, what the hell?

What! You're Talking Again

Three strikes in a baseball game mean you're out at home plate. Just a minute! A strike at the workplace means you're out of a job, which may result in no food on your plate at home.

In most sports, you must score to win the game. After a date, the fellas want to know if you scored? That's how you play the game.

Hey, Honey, I need to hit the can before we leave. Campbell soup or Progressive?

If a plane is grounded that means it can't fly. He'll go far in life because he's grounded. Wait! What?

I decided not to participate, so don't hold your breath. Why should I hold my breath? I'll die.

Oh God, I can't believe this! Wait! What? Who are you talking to, me or God?

Let's get a jump on things. So, you want me to jump on everything and break it?

I got my eye on you. You mean to tell me you pulled your eyeball out of its socket and placed it in my lap?

Have you ever visited someone in prison and upon leaving you told them to have a nice day? Have a nice day….in prison?

Hold your horses, I'll be with you in a second. I live in Manhattan next to Mr. Rogers not Mr. Ed. By the way, has a second passed yet?

Are we there yet? You tell me.

Martin Had a Dream

Martin, wake up from that dream

Books are being banned

Is this Nazi Germany? No! it's Florida, no it's Texas

Martin, wake up from that dream

They only want power

They only sell fear

They only respect money

Martin, wake up from that dream

Jim Crow, Jim Jordan, Marjorie Taylor Green

Arm the teachers

Martin, wake up from that dream

They tell me what to say, where to live, who to worship, who to be

Martin, wake up from that dream, by any means necessary

Martin, are you awake? Tell me about your dream

It was a nightmare

Defiance

I am rhythm, I am rhyme, I am plain-spoken

I am change, I am different, I am not your token

I am free, I am he, I am me

I will not conform, I reject thee

You are not my savior, you are not my boss

Burn me at the stake, nail me to the cross

Knowledge is my spear, defiance is my shield

I am here, I am strong, I am real

We're All Aliens

Ellis Silver, PhD wrote a book called "Humans Are Not from Earth." He listed seven reasons why he believe that we are not indigenous to Mother Earth. Of course, I added my own twist to it. I think you will find this interesting.

1. We look so different: with the lack of hair, our bodies don't adjust to climate change. We freeze in the winter and burn in the summer. Every warm-blooded animal has some kind of fur or feathers to protect the outer layer of the skin. Humans do not. Also, we have four limbs, yet we walk on two of them 100% of the time. No other animal with four limbs walks on two limbs 100% of the time.

2. We are too advanced: compared to the other animals on Earth, we are too smart. Humans invent things and have the capacity to speak and learn multiple languages. Can you imagine a zebra explaining to a lion why he shouldn't eat him?

3. We can't sleep: Scientists have proven that the human's circadian rhythm is not twenty-four hours. Instead, it's twenty-five hours, suggesting that the planet we come from has a twenty-five-hour rotation. This is why we can't get a good night's sleep.

4. Rapid overpopulation: because we have no natural predators, we exist outside the ecosystem. No other animal population in its own ecosystem has grown faster than humans.

5. We don't like it here: we alter the planet to fit us, not the other way around. We have difficulties living in the natural world, so we terraform it. We also can't eat most of the food on Earth unless we alter it in some way.

6. Earth is our prison: we were left here because we are unable to exist with other higher beings. We have traits that other animals and higher beings do not have, such as greed, lust, vengeance, envy, pride, and a need to be entertained.

7. We are an experiment: Just imagine, we were placed in different locations and climates on the Earth just to see what we would do to survive. Yet, we've been told by religion that humans will eventually leave the Earth. Here are some quotes; "When you die, you're going to a better place," "Jesus is coming back for the righteous", "You will leave this place and venture to the spirit realm", and "You will be rewarded in Heaven (or somewhere else)". Whatever the quote, they all reference not being here on Mother Earth. Maybe those scientists who placed us here, promise to return one day when

we've learned our lesson. Maybe we mistaken our transporters for celestial gods as they departed toward the skies waving goodbye? Maybe? Well, that's it for me…. Scottie, beam me up.

Left Behind

Remember Kirk Cameron? He was a child television star on the sitcom Growing Pains from 1985 to 1992. As Kirk grew older, he became an Evangelist, film Producer and Director. Each of his B-rated films were related to his belief in Christianity. He created and directed a film called Left Behind. This film told the story of the biblical rapture and what happened to those humans who were left on Earth for the next seven years.

In the film, there was a rebel group of people determined to expose the anti-Christ to the world. The anti-Christ happened to be the President of the World. After due diligence and clever planning, the rebels were able to expose the anti-Christ during his televised State-of-the-Union address. The rebels rejoiced and celebrated their victory, knowing they had saved the world. To their surprise, the world didn't care. People only cared about their own well-being. And if that wasn't changed, they accepted the anti-Christ's vision of living, knowing that their souls would be condemned forever.

This movie reminds me of today's reality in the United States. American prides itself on the peaceful transition of power. It prides itself on upholding the Constitution as the law of the land. The Presidents pride themselves on representing all Americans with dignity, honesty, and being presidential. Not the case with Donald Trump and his followers.

All Americans saw what happened on January 6th; the attack on the Capital, the disregard of the Constitution by a U.S. President, the perpetrated lies implemented by Trump's political followers, and the silence of the vast majority of the Republican Party. Millions of Americans didn't care.

Donald Trump gave a speech at the Black Conservative Federation Conference. He stated, Black people can relate to him because he has a criminal mug shot. As he looked at the audience with the glaring lights in his eyes. He also stated, he could not see the White people, but he can see the Black people just find. But what was more surprising is those statements were met with thundering applause by Blacks in the audience and the Black hosts. Amazing!

Immigrants are poisoning the blood of America; they didn't care. Trying to ban Muslims from entering America; they didn't care. There were good people on both sides; they didn't care. Wanting to grab a woman's crouch on audio; they didn't care. Found guilty of sexual assault in a civil case; they didn't care. I guess the only thing "they" care about is putting Donald Trump back in power, for reasons unknown.

The question I would have for Trump followers is: What did you leave behind? Did you leave behind the truth? Did you leave behind dignity? Did you leave behind humanity for others? Did you leave behind the rule of law?

Or did you leave behind your soul?

Personality

If you were raised by robots, who would you be? If the environment did not provide any human contact or experiences, would you develop your own personality based on your parent's DNA? Can you develop your own? Or, will you be a carbon copy of your father, mother, or a combination of both?

Is the world different today, because personalities are different from yesteryear?

Five or six decades ago, it was common knowledge that, if you talked back to your parents with attitude, expect a hard right hand to the head or backend. In today's world its "time out." I believe the difference then versus today, is fear versus possession. In some cases, fear of something can lead to respect. I also believe that the fear of pain or rejection can block the growth of a personality. The lack of possession can lead to anger or desperation.   Or, maybe the desire to want even more? Both factors add to the foundation of a personality. Of course, there are many factors that make a person who they are. But your reaction to a situation at a young age, may give some indication how you would respond to situations at an older age.

What makes a strong personality versus a weak personality?   I guess you would have to define strong and weak before the conclusion? Dr. Martin Luther King Jr. told us to turn the other cheek. Malcolm X told us not to turn the cheek, but to defend yourself with any means necessary. In my view they both had strong personalities, but with different views. Martin nor Malcolm appeared fearful. Is there something else that moles the personality to rise above others?

Is a personality the way you act, sound, or look? Webster Dictionary describes personality as the quality of a "person." What about animals? We love our pets because of their personality. Is this something humans and animals share? What was Noah Webster's personality? What is your personality?

- 50% of all U.S. citizens are mixed race.
- There is a coast-to-coast border wall between the US and Mexico.
- Each state's Constitution overrides the U.S. Constitution regarding immigration.
- In Texas: armed militia groups are licensed by the state to enforce immigration laws. There have been approximately 9000 deaths of undocumented people when encountering the militias.
- The U.S. remains a military power in the world. However, it's fourth behind China, the European Union, and South America regarding economic power.
- Realizing their similarity in culture, language, and vast resources of energy. Every country in South America unite as one country. It's known as the country of M.I.N. (Mayan-Inka Nation).
- The European Union banned all immigration from African and the Middle Eastern countries. Laws were passed to preserve each countries individual language, culture, and race.
- The peso shares the same value as the dollar.
- There are 6-to-10-bedroom apartments, because the average rent is $10,000 a month.
- Churches and other religious institutions must pay taxes.
- The average high temperature is 80 degrees Fahrenheit...in Alaska!
- The Florida Keys are completely underwater.
- New vehicles are so expensive that the loan payoff is twenty years.
- There's a statue of Taylor Swift in Kansas City.
- The art of crocheting is lost in time.
- Pets can be written off as a dependent on your tax form.
- The John Lewis Voting Rights Act was finally passed.

Vader

For those of us who attended church at a young age, we were taught when our love ones pass away, we would see them again in heaven. And that we would be united with all those who believe and followed the same biblical set of rules, to ensure our entry into the golden gates. What's funny, I often say to myself: "There's no way I want to be with certain family members and others I don't necessarily care for, for eternity."

When my pet rabbit (Vader) passed away, I literally cried for three days. I thought about the eternal heavenly garden described in other faiths. My feelings and thoughts at that time; imagined my rabbit hopping towards me, standing on his two hind legs while leaning against my thigh as I kneeled, surrounded by a beautiful garden with no people around. No pearly gates, no Saint Peters greeting me wearing a toga, no golden brick roads. Just Vader. Eventually, I would see other love ones I prefer, but I want to see my rabbit first.

For most of us, our pets are family. For some of us, our pets are our children. They don't follow any religious guideline and yet they give us unconditional love. Do we want to spend eternity with our beloved pets too? Of course we do. Now that's heaven!